SmackDown

by Will Sherman

Title: SmackDown

Author: Will Sherman

Published by: Will Sherman

First Edition, April 2018,

Published in the United States of America

ISBN-13: 978-1981651542

ISBN-10: 1981651543

SmackDown

WILL SHERMAN

First Edition

April 2018

By Will Sherman

Foreword

The most powerful ideas are almost always the simple ones. But like most things in life worth having, it takes more than an idea (a vision), it takes disciplined action and day to day execution to realize the potential of your idea or vision. Will Sherman's "SmackDown" is a testament to both of these axioms.

For the last 30 years of my career in the Real Estate Industry, one constant has remained **-- the sales professional on the front line has more to do with the success of a community and ultimately the company, than any single factor.**

Executives work tirelessly in strategic meetings pouring over data to put together the best offerings based up "Product – Price & Positioning" for the specific location. Additionally, sincere efforts are implemented to best advertise and market the product and community so that on-site sales professionals can achieve the anticipated results. However, time and time again, executives (at least the truly good ones) realize that the disciplined efforts of the sales professional makes the difference.

Depending upon the market cycle and individual company philosophies, expectations vary as to how much traffic should be driven by the company verses driven by the on-site sales professional.

Notwithstanding the difference in expectations, one fact is consistent – **the more exposure and traffic you create, the better results you will achieve.**

As you read this book, you'll probably have the same reaction as I did. "Why doesn't every sales professional utilize these proven activities?". The answer is that as the author Will Sherman has discovered in his many years of becoming a true sales professional – **it's not the idea, it's the execution!**

Enjoy learning the insights in Smackdown and more importantly make the commitment to create the "Discipline" to become "Consistent, Predictable and Accountable" for your success. If and when you do, the sky is the limit.

Ken Trainer

President/COO, Chesmar Homes

SmackDown

Contents

PART 1

What is "SmackDown"?

What is "SmackDown"?

First off, let's discuss what SmackDown IS NOT.

- SmackDown is NOT a system that will teach you high pressure sales techniques or unethical tactics.
- SmackDown is NOT going to eliminate the need for you to work hard.
- SmackDown is NOT the only effective strategy you should employ.

Now that we know what SmackDown isn't, we can start looking at what it IS.

- SmackDown is a proven and tested system for increasing traffic and sales.
- SmackDown is a comprehensive strategy focusing on multiple aspects of marketing and sales, this contrasts with most strategies that will focus on one or two components and neglect other potential prospect streams.
- Although the title of this book references social media in particular, we will cover much more than that.

SmackDown is the knowledge I have accumulated over the years: knowledge I've acquired from working with people in the industry, the many books I've read or observations I've made and also ideas that have worked and not worked for me.

SmackDown IS your User's Manual for Real Estate Sales. Simply put, SmackDown is a list of various effective things you can do to get the maximum results from your real estate marketing efforts. As a real estate professional, your goal is to get prospective clients into your office, to have potential customers to notice you, to get customers to come to you and interested in what you have to offer. But once you have their attention, you must capitalize on it. This is when you can present what you have for them. This is where the SmackDown comes into play. My entire system is designed to help anyone in the real estate industry whether you are an experienced new home sales agent, a real estate agent, or a sales manager. Let this be your user's manual for optimizing your social media efforts for real estate sales. As a current sales agent for a new home builder in Texas, I have tried numerous strategies and have both succeeded and failed. While it is important for you to understand my point of view, I also want you to know that the principles I review in this book, with slight tweaking, can be applied to any field. After all, a large part of the SmackDown system consists of techniques I employed before I was even in the real estate industry.

How the concepts that are a part of the SmackDown strategy were conceived and how they have evolved is just as important as understanding how the SmackDown system works. It is extremely important to always know why you are doing

4

something and not just what you are doing. "The why" is probably the most important part of the puzzle.

Many years ago, I was a Fitness Manager at Gold's Gym. My two main responsibilities were to make sure my staff of trainers were knowledgeable in all aspects of fitness and effective in selling these skills to prospective clients. This is where I first came up with what I call the "Circle of Service." This concept is where the entire SmackDown system eventually evolved from.

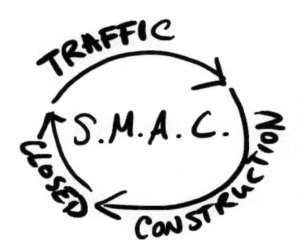

The Circle of Service is the life cycle of your prospects/customers. Prospects will enter different stages of the life cycle during the process of buying a home (see graphic to the above) and each stage requires you to interact with them differently.

Identifying each stage of this life cycle allows you to identify strategies that will positively impact the likelihood of turning the prospect into an actual customer, remaining a customer, and ultimately referring more customers to you.

Years of brainstorming new ideas, experimenting to find out what does or doesn't work, and learning from others in the industry has resulted in having a list of strategies that have proven to be effective for me in one way or another. Even now I am constantly trying new ways to do things that are being added to this list. This list is what I have come to call the "SmackDown Checklist."

CHAPTER 1

The SmackDown List

The term "SmackDown" is an acronym and unlike the title of the book, is spelled differently, It's SMaC. The letters each mean something specific. Each item on the SmackDown list must meet 3 criteria.

"S" stands for specific. It stands for things I'm going to *specifically* do. I'm not just going to say, "I'm working on social media." I'm actually going to say, "This week I'm doing a Facebook boosted post. That boosted post is going to be "promoting my inventory home" or it's going to focus on "selling the corner lot." Or it might be I'm going to put out bandits on Friday and Sunday." (We will cover bandit signs later in this book). It's going to be extremely specific. An list of specific action

7

items that you are going to accomplish in a set time frame.

Lets look at it this way; say you have a ship and the ship doesn't have a captain to steer it. It's just going to set sail in a random direction. How likely is it to get to its destination? Now, say you have a ship that's got a captain. That captain has a direct course set. That ship is probably going to get to where it needs to go. So, the more you have a specific goal, a specific way or plan to get there, the more likely you are to get to that destination. This system is designed to be that defined direct course.

'M' stands for methodical. Methodical means that you're employing these specific techniques for a reason. You've actually spent some time researching and have a pretty good idea as to how the general public will respond to your ideas. You're optimistic when you exercise these methods that your work will result in you selling another house or bettering the experience of someone that is already buying a home from you. You have a defined reason for your action. You are just not standing around waving your arms and hoping something's going to work.

This also means using the information you gather from the results of your actions to either double down, modify or even abandon your marketing efforts. You must always consider adapting your method to drive the best results.

'C' stands for consistent. You must employ your specific and methodical strategies consistently. You don't just want to try a technique once and when or if it doesn't work the first time, decide you are never going to do it again. If you're trying the SmackDown strategies consistently, your results should eventually flow like water out of a water pump. When you first start pumping water it may take a little bit of time for the water to come out. But eventually something is going to drip. The more consistently you pump, the more consistently water flows. If you stop pumping, the water eventually stops flowing.

So, what typically would stop someone from pumping the water? They get either frustrated or they get complacent. They either see no results right away and give up or the opposite, they get a few people, a few clients, a few sales and it seems the water's pumping on its own, so they slow down or stop pumping and suddenly, the water stops. These people are left scratching their heads wondering why, but if they just stop and think about it, they will realize they stopped pumping, they stopped doing the things that brought the people to them. And then when they try to play catch up, they are basically starting and stopping, starting and stopping, which is never efficient. **Momentum is harder to build and easier to maintain.**

I have worked with people who have this issue where they had a spurt of success. They sell two or three homes in a row. They get some great commissions. They start taking time off, their attention and focus is on things other than sales and they stop doing anything that would lead to future business. Then, when those sales finish, suddenly they are left in this massive hole with no leads.

CHAPTER 2

Six Months: Ten Million Dollars

The subtitle of the book mentions the six months and ten million dollars that motivated me to write this book, but the truth is, I had been doing these things for quite some time and had been extremely successful using the SmackDown strategies well before the time I put my pen down on paper. But since I had no "control subject" to compare my work to, I never realized how effective my strategy was to alternatives. Truthfully, I never really even looked at it as a "system" or strategy, I just thought it was a list of things I did that were just a part of my job. I figured these were things commonly done by people that had jobs similar to mine

Boy was I wrong!

In September of 2014 came the perfect case study. The

company I currently work for had two communities both similar in location, demographic, price range and both offering the same floor plans. Both had also been struggling for quite some time. I took over one of these communities and started employing the SmackDown strategies. The results were staggering!

My community had just shy of ten million in a six-month stretch while the other community had sold just one home during the same six-months. I then looked at other builders in the same area to see if maybe there were other factors that led to our results and most of the other builders were in the one to two million range or less which was more consistent with the comparison community I was using to compare my community to.

What was my conclusion? SmackDown works!

CHAPTER 3

The Foundation

Before we get into the meat and potatoes of this book we must first make sure you have a good foundation to start from. This foundation is an understanding of how to use the SmackDown system so that you know how to implement and adapt the system towards the results you are seeing.

You need to think of every marketing effort as an experiment. Just like an experiment, it will have a cause and an effect. If you don't look for the effect, you don't know if what you are doing is effective at all. You don't want to just do things and not weigh the results, you will never know if what you are doing is working or if it's a total waste of time and possibly even a waste of money. It is very easy to identify the results of your work, for the most part. The different social media platforms will illustrate stats and graphics to show the efficiency of your posts and advertisements.

Paying attention to this data is crucial but is only half of the picture. Your goal in analyzing this data is to get people to contact you or come to your place of business. So, if you aren't asking the people that call, email or show up at your door how they found you, then you are missing out on the most important piece of data you could have, which the social networks won't be able to tell you!

Let's use one scenario as an example. If you have a social media post and a marketing email that are sent out around the same time with similar content and you see the social media post getting a large amount of interaction online but you get no responses to the email you sent out, it would be easy to assume that the social media post was more effective. But what if the two people who called you and the three people who walked into your office today, asking for you, were people that saw the email? Unless you ask you them how they found you, you may never know that the email you sent was much more effective than the social media post that merely generated some "likes."

The strategy is simple, do the things on the SmackDown list consistently, pay attention to your results and modify your strategy based on said results.

PART 2

The Practice

CHAPTER 4

The Checklist

The SmackDown system is broken down into the following categories.

    I.   Signage

    II.   Real Estate Agents

    III.   Referrals

    IV.   Social Media

    V.   Info Tubes and Flyers

    VI.   The Community Experience

    VII.   Trade Outs

    VIII.   Follow up

I. Signage

Bandit Signs

Bandit signs are small signs, usually placed in high traffic areas, such as intersections or maybe entrances to communities. The signs are used to get prospective clients attention and generate a response or lead someone to your location. These signs typically have a low cost. I have used bandit signs in two different ways to target two different demographics. But whichever way you utilize them, they need to follow a few simple rules. They need to be short, sweet, to the point and placed strategically where it is most beneficial for the desired response.

Method 1

Method 1 is best used for lower priced homes with buyers who are more price and payment sensitive. Bandits are placed at busy intersections near the community with the desired response of people seeing them and calling. The homes that I was selling at the time were low in price and the lower the price, the larger the market. Since the buyers looking in the lower price ranges are more payment and down payment sensitive the bandit I used said *'$800 a month, zero down, new home'* and had my phone number on it. Somebody looking for a $500,000 home is probably not going to call after seeing that type of bandit because they know that the house they're looking for is not going to cost as little as $800 a month.

Each time I did this I would literally have over one hundred phone calls per day in the first few days. Please keep in mind many of the people that will call this type of sign typically had bad credit and low income. You will have to talk to many people before you will get to one that has the ability to purchase from you. But if you are struggling for traffic and business, what do you have to lose?

A few years later I moved to a community where the homes were much more expensive. In theory I could have used the same strategy and had a bandit with the higher price, in my new neighborhood, but if I put *$50,000 down, $3,000 a month* with my phone number, it's probably not going to have a very big impact. Therefore, I didn't continue to use that practice in my new and more expensive neighborhood.

Method 2

This method is effective for lower priced communities as well as higher priced communities. Instead of totally abandoning bandit signs in the higher priced community, I looked for an alternative way to use them. At the front of my neighborhood, I have bandits that feature green arrows on a nice-looking background that point into the neighborhood. These signs help people to find us and depending on my demographic, will also include some details regarding our homes or the community itself, such as *acre lots* or *four car garages*. In this case, I am using language that will appeal to the people who fit the target demographic of the higher priced homes I am trying to sell. By including this language, I'm just modifying a technique that has worked for me in the past for a new market. Instead of

abandoning the whole principle of it, I created a different way of doing the same thing.

When choosing what words or graphics to put on the signs, you should always look at what will appeal to your target demographic. What is special about what you have to offer? What is it that you have that others don't? These things are your strengths, focus on those things in all the marketing you do. If it's a feature that you offer, you want to put this feature on the bandit. If it's a low price you have the flexibility to get down to, you want to include that. Maybe you have a special offer for veterans or you're able to offer special loans that don't require a down payment. Whatever it is, make sure people know about it.

With any advertising, you basically have a few seconds to get somebody's attention. You want those few seconds to be effective. Your advertising needs to be appealing and to the point. It needs to be a message that captures potential clients' attention immediately.

You can experiment with bandit signs by using different graphics and language and noting your influx of calls. Two weeks down the road you can put up a sign with a different message and take note of how many calls come in. If one sign generates more interest than another, you can stick with the sign that works for you. That is the market telling you what it wants. You should never assume you know what people want. Half of what will make a bandit sign effective is what you are saying. The other half is where you are saying it. For example, I put bandits at intersections near a highway once and I didn't get any calls. I found out later it was because the city limits begin near the highway and they have a no bandit sign policy.

Right after I put them down, the city picked them all up. It wasn't the message that was not effective; it was that the message was no longer there due to my placement. If I hadn't checked back, I wouldn't have known.

Another piece of the location puzzle is the distance from your location. Usually I like to post the signs within a five-mile radius of your location. People who see these signs likely work or shop in your area. If they don't already live in the area, they might be thinking about it.

If you are a real estate agent and you don't have a specific community you always work in, you could place signs at busy intersections in the nicer parts of whatever area you know best. You can still promote a price like in the way we used the bandits in Method 1. The only difference is when someone calls you, you should ask them exactly what they are looking for in a home and then use your MLS (a listing service used by real estate agents) to find a home that meets their criteria. Some of the people that call may also have a home to sell, so if you are a real estate agent you may end up with a listing on the home they need to sell as well as helping them find the new home they are calling about!

Getting the bandits placed is probably the hardest part. I have experimented with people putting them out for me and with me putting them up myself. The time that it takes for me to put them up is costly, so I've hired companies to do it for me. I use Google to find local people who specialize in creating bandit signs and bandit sign placement. Sure, there have been situations where I couldn't find anybody, but in those cases, I contacted the local Boy-Scout troops and offered a troop donation in exchange for their time. It's going to take you so much time to place the signs yourself, especially if you place them at numerous major intersections. If you're putting them around your neighborhood, though, you're probably only dealing with five to ten signs, which would probably take you about 30 minutes to post.

If you are using Method 1 by placing bandit signs at busy intersections, I would put at least 100-250. I suggest every intersection close to you and targeting the most congested areas. I was in areas of Houston where thousands of people pass intersections daily. In this case, we typically have up to ten bandits at each intersection. You want to make sure you have them facing each direction of traffic at the intersection.

As far as cost, 200 signs probably cost around $300-$400 depending on how much someone charges you to place them. Double sided signs are more expensive than single sided. But keep in mind, you don't really need double sided when traffic is only going one way.

Let's say for example, you spend $300-$500 on these signs and you only sell one house. That one house more than paid for the effort and the cost.

Billboards

A billboard is a larger and much more expensive version of a bandit. If you are spending money on a billboard, in my opinion, it needs to say something that will really be attention grabbing. A short, clear and compelling message will make it effective and increase your chances of getting your money's worth. Having a clear and compelling message is something you will hear me talk about time and time again, this is where I see a huge amount of wasted time and money. If you just put the name of your company up there, that's about brand recognition, and although over time that will help your company be recognized, it's not going to help you sell a house right now.

You need to say: **This is who I am. This is what I have to offer. Come here and get this.** Or something like **"Buy a house, get a pool!"** It's something simple, something powerful, and something that suits your demographic.

Let's say, for example, my homes start at x price point, if my price point is a strength then I would use that info on the billboard. If my price point is not a strength, then I definitely would not put the price on there. If I offer four car garages standard, that's a strength. I'm a big fan of putting phone numbers on billboards along with maybe two or three bullet points highlighting your strengths. Keep in mind, people are more likely to call while they are in the car. They are less likely to email or visit your website while driving, especially if it's a long address that's difficult to remember. People usually think, "I will email them later, but I might call right now." If they are calling because of a billboard that is close by, you might be able to talk to them and have them visit the listing while they are still in the area.

Billboards need to be as close to your neighborhood as possible so that your audience is relevant and familiar with the neighborhood – the advertisement should help direct people to your location. To get the most value out of a billboard advertisement, they should be located near major intersections and major highways, essentially locations with high traffic. If people don't see your signs, they don't know who or where you are. The billboard should include a line about location, such as *a mile down on the left*, or *a mile this way*, or *turn now*. If the billboard is located right before your neighborhood, it might say *turn right in half a mile*.

Banners

Banners are pretty easy to figure out. They are large signs you can put up near your place of business. Let's say you're having a grand opening and you have a fence in your backyard and the side of it faces a major road. Why not have a banner on it that says,

"Grand Opening" or "Closeout Sale—4 Lots Left" or "Open House"? That grabs people's attention.

To summarize, if you lack signage you will most likely lack customers. If they are not aware you are nearby, they will not know to come to visit you. Also, one important thing to remember is the signage you have needs to be checked constantly. Your prices or other offerings might change, and you want your signage to reflect the correct information.

II. Real Estate Agents

There are many things you can do to generate real estate agent traffic in your neighborhood and make sure the ones who do come, keep coming back.

The first thing is to treat the agents the way they want to be treated. Let's say you have an agent who is going through a process with you of building a home for a client. You need to make sure you're updating the agent, including them in the process. If you're updating the buyer on the status of their home, but not updating the real estate agent, the agent will feel they're in a position where they know less about their client's home than the client does, and that's not a good position for an agent to be in. The fact that most salespeople do not update and include the agent will really help you differentiate yourself from your competition. This warm and inclusive treatment will stick with your agents and will ensure that you stick in the front of their mind. If they have a new client and simultaneously receive an update from you, they are more likely to bring that business to you. We have all heard the expression "out of sight, out of mind," which definitely applies here. The sales person that does not update the agent is not the salesperson that the agent will most likely think of.

Since you want more agents to bring you clients, you need to make sure they're aware you exist and know what you have to offer. One simple way you can do this is by visiting their offices. Each time I visit a new real estate office I bring flyers that detail my available inventory and the floor plans I can build as well as community info. Once I am in the office, I find the office manager and ask if I can bring breakfast to one of their weekly meetings and give a five to ten-minute presentation.

The presentations have been extremely effective for me in generating traffic. Usually, the things that I have to offer are so exciting, and the way I do business is so different, that it's something that's appealing to them. This presentation is where you will outline the strengths of your community, what makes you different and better than everyone else. If you only go in there and just give out flyers and say "please come and see us" you won't get much of a response. I've had numerous instances where the agents in the presentations end up buying homes from us. Right now, I have a real estate broker and two real estate agents building homes with us, and it's because they saw the difference in what we have to offer. When they're building homes with us, that's the ultimate testimony to their customers; I can almost guarantee you that if it's a positive experience, they're going to be bring you more business. I try to visit at least one real estate office per week to drop off flyers and information and try to schedule at least two presentations per month. While you visit their offices, it's a good idea to pick up all of the agents' business cards that work through that real estate office. That way you can get their emails and contact info and plug it into your other marketing efforts such as Constant Contact (a mass email program that we will get to later in this book).

To find the real estate offices nearest to me, I've used Google, searching for: "real estate brokerage," "real estate office," or for the big names in the industry, "Century 21" for example. Google usually generates their phone numbers and addresses so you can find them easily. I usually just print out the search page and just cross off the ones I've visit as I go down the list. I might spend $25, $50, or maybe $100 on food or gift cards that I bring to the presentations, obviously depending on the size of the brokerage.

The main idea is you're bringing them something that they appreciate and in exchange they're giving you their time.

MLS is a property listing service.

In most cities and large areas like counties, suburban areas, metropolitan areas, there will be a home listing service. For example, in Houston we had "Houston Area Realtors" or "www.HAR.com." If a lot of people, whether they have real estate or the prospects themselves, turn to that source, or others like "www.realtor.com" or whatever the listing service is, you must make sure you are listed there. That's where a lot of people turn to find homes; and that's where the traffic is. If you aren't listed there, you do not exist to the people that use these sites as their source to find homes.

So how do get your homes on there? Real estate agents will typically have access to their local MLS, so you would need to either be one or use one. Probably the first thing a real estate agent learns is how to list a home on MLS. There's quite a few things that go into a typical listing; pictures of the home, the home's specifications such as the square footage of the home and room sizes, tax info, school info and much more. Whether you are listing or using an agent to list your homes, you need to make sure you are putting your best foot forward by having captivating pictures, accurate information and extensive descriptions of the home and its features. You'd be surprised how many agents have posted a photo of the front of the clients' home, and there are two cars in the driveway, or the grass isn't mowed, or the photo is blurry or it's just a bad quality photo. Why would you do that?

If you want someone to come see your home, you must show them a photo that's appealing to them. The photos you post are the first impressions someone will have of that home, so if your photos give a bad impression, why would they ever want to come to see you? The people combing through these listings are probably looking at listing after listing and waiting for something to jump out at them. Make sure your listing is the one that jumps out the furthest.

If you are not an agent you may not be creating the listing yourself, so if you hire an agent to list it for you, you are the quality control. You're the one who goes back and says, "this listing is good enough or not good enough," or "this description is good enough or not good enough," or "you failed to mention this feature or this other thing, let's make sure we do." You simply want to make sure you are making a great first impression by putting your best foot forward.

You also need to make sure your listings show up accurately in map searches. Every once in a while, the little pin on the map drops in the wrong place, which can mislead the prospective client looking at where you are located. This happened to me recently, the map was showing that one of my homes, valued at almost $500,000 was located in a trailer park! Obviously, that was not going to help me sell that home.

If you've had no luck selling the listed home, I suggest changing the photos and price on the listing periodically. The new price and pictures may attract the attention of someone who had already looked at the listing to look at it again.

"Ghost Homes"

This is a term and a strategy I recently started using that has generated impressive results. My goal is always to determine what the market wants and to try not to assume I already know. In order to do that, I list most of my floor plans online in my local MLS service. When doing this I list homes that have not yet started construction. I use professional photos of the same floor plan the last time we built it so that anyone that looks at the listing can get a mental image of the finished product. Obviously model home photos are going to be more appealing since they are typically staged well. I also make sure to include in the photo description that the photos are of a model or home that has the same floor plan but is not the actual subject listed. The pictures will show some features or selections that will vary from the actual subject. I also make absolutely sure to note that the home has not yet started and will be done in "5 to 7 months" or whatever the timeframe might be.

My original plan was to leave a variety of plans online for a few weeks and see which ones generated the most calls and interest, which was ultimately my strategy to find what the market at the time was most interested in. Once I determined which of the listings generated the most interest, I was going to start building that floor plan. But since the listings gave me a steady flow of interested clients, I decided to leave them online to capitalize on this new strategy. Obviously, I came up with the term "ghost home" or "ghost listing" because the home isn't built just yet, but is still listed.

There are a couple things to remember with this strategy. You will eventually get calls from people that do not fully read the listing that think the listing is for a home that is completely finished. They sometimes get annoyed with the fact that the home has not started yet, but I do remind the prospective buyer that all this information is disclosed in the listing. Anyone that calls, whether it's a real estate agent with a client or a potential home buyer themselves, I let them know that the listing is for a home that has not yet started and will be finished in "5 to 7 months" or whatever the timeframe would be to build it. I ask them if they need something that is completely finished and invite them to see some other homes I may have that fit their needs. If they don't necessarily need something that's finished, I will talk to them about building the plan they called about or maybe a plan that might better fit their needs. As I write this book, my most recent sale is from one of my current ghost listings.

Every three months or so, you need to make sure you terminate and relist your ghost homes. This is for a couple reasons, first and more importantly when a new home is listed most MLS services will send out an alert to real estate agents and potential home buyers. This "new listing" will get seen by more people than one that is a few months old. Secondly the fact that the listing says the home will be ready in a certain number of months, but is a few months old, will cause prospective clients to see red flags when they see how old the listing is.

BTSA's

In Texas, and possibly elsewhere, you can put a bonus or what is commonly referred to as a "BTSA" (Bonus to Selling Agent) on a home. This means if an agent brings a buyer to you, and that buyer buys a home from you, you can give the agent a bonus for helping sell this house by a certain date or at a certain price. You can say if the buyer buys it above a certain asking price, then the agent gets a $2000 bonus, or a $5000 bonus, or whatever. Or if the home closes before a certain date, it has a specific bonus. You can put an advertisement out to local offices, put it on MLS, or an email blast to local real estate agents that says, "$5,000 bonus". Obviously, this strategy would need to be approved by whoever you are selling the home for, whether you work for a builder or are an agent selling a home for the owner, the money ultimately will come out of their pockets.

In my experience it is more effective to take this money off of the home price to make it more attractive to the potential homebuyer than it is using it towards a BTSA but as always, it may be more or less effective in other markets.

III. Referrals

Referrals, the best type of traffic you can get.

A referral typically comes from somebody who had a good experience with something that you have to offer and, therefore, recommends somebody to you. A person who is referred to you is ten times more likely to buy from you than someone who was not referred.

The main idea behind referrals is constantly setting the expectation that they are appreciated; and somewhat expected.

One of the first things you should ask a prospective client is how they heard about you, and ask if they were referred. Let them know that a majority of people who walk through the door have been referred by somebody else. Explain you are only asking because you just want to make sure you recognize the people who referred them, if indeed they were referred to you. **This puts the idea in their mind that they might at some point refer someone to you themselves.** This is one of the first things I do when someone first comes into my model home.

Another effective way to promote referrals is what I refer to as my "blank check" promotion. During the contract the new buyers are given a couple blank checks. The checks will not have a name on them but will have an amount on them along with our logo. If that person gives them to someone and they come in with it, they will both get a discount on the upgrades of their home for the amount that is on that check split between them. The amount can be taken out of your normal incentive money or however you see fit. These checks will help to both set the expectation for referrals but also help remind clients about the referral bonus, if they happen to see the blank checks lying around in a kitchen drawer.

Whatever method or promotion you use to promote referrals, the key is always making sure both parties know how much you appreciate the referral and that you will take care of anyone that they send to you.

A lot of the times referrals will automatically happen if you use the SmackDown program correctly and consistently.

From time to time somebody will see a Facebook post of a friend building with you and come in. That wasn't really the person going to them and saying "you need to go see this person," but we still see it as a referral. The business was generated due to the fact this person bought something from you. When spending time with customers, you don't want to come across as a "used-car dealer" and be pushy about them referring someone to you. Frankly you need to earn the referral before you can really start asking for it. And once you feel like you have, just keep planting the seed and sometimes even joke around with them about it. It should be something you mention every once in a while, but not something that's the topic of every conversation.

Another key to referrals is to make sure you are always in the back of their minds, that way when someone talks about buying a home you are always the person that comes to mind.

You want to try to stay in touch with people that you have done business in the past with as well. But you want to do it without bothering them or interrupting their lives. A simple way is to send a postcard on the anniversary of them buying their home. It can say, "Hey, I hope you guys are doing okay. Let us know if you ever need anything." At the bottom of it, just say "Let us know if any friends or family need our services." That way asking for a referral is not intrusive.

Another strategy is to remind them of the home's maintenance milestones. You could let them know at the end of the first year; "They need to look for warranty items", or "File for their homestead exemption." This reminder means you're offering something to them, and showing you're still invested in your relationship.

When I was selling homes in Bay Town, I had a younger couple who came in and wanted to buy a home. They were really excited about the things we had to offer, and then I gave them the second folder. Literally, within a few hours, they had brought their parents to us. Their parents bought a home on the spot and the kids ended up buying a little bit later because they had to sell their other home first. I can't say that they wouldn't have bought or brought their parents to us had I not given the second folder, but I at least know for a fact that I did it and I planted the seed and it happened

.

IV. Social Media

As of the writing of this book, I have been in home sales for over ten years. During this time, social media has completely changed the business landscape. In today's age, a lot of people, especially the younger demographic, spend a large amount of time on social media. In fact, the younger the age group; the lower the price point, the more time they spend on social media. It is an entire online world that they live in, and if you're not in that world, you simply don't exist.

Age groups have a lot to do with which social media platform they're using and what they use it for. So, in turn, this also influences which platform will be most effective for you and how you use it. Initially, when social media first hit the scene, I think it's something most people saw as a small niche market. But as that niche has gotten larger, it's no longer a niche. It is now an entire demographic to target, and eventually it's going to be everybody.

I've heard some interesting statistics about millennials currently in their 20s and 30s. By 2020, it's estimated that 46% of the workforce will be millennials. That's 46% percent of people earning money and making buying decisions. By 2025, it's going to be 86%. The stats on how much time this demographic spends online versus being active in the real world are unbelievable and will continue to impact business.

In January 2014, I attended a sales training given by Steve Rigby, who has been one of the biggest influences in my life. He produced a training program focusing on positivity and treating people the way that they want to be treated. His system focuses on creating a better experience for your customers. It does this by focusing on being a better person. Steve suggests that by "being a better person," prospective clients will recognize this and know that you truly want to help them.

Before I went to Steve's training, I was the type of sales person who operated more like a used-car salesman. I was more of a "slam them when they're in the door" or "this is the last day for this sale" sort of salesperson.

I left Steve's training with an entirely different outlook on life. Within that year, I read 28 books and created new life goals. I wanted to become better and more successful in many areas of my life, and my career was one of the facets I wanted to improve.

When I hit the books, I generated a ton of knowledge that I interpreted and modified to fit my model for success. A lot of the insights I gleaned from this research, I'm sharing in this book. During this time, I worked in a community in a small Texas town outside of Houston called Baytown. The city itself is full of and surrounded by refineries as it is on the Gulf coast, where a lot of oil companies do a large portion of their offshore drilling. Before going through Steve's training, I had issues with customer retention. In the 1-2 years before the training I had somewhere around a 20-30% cancellation rate. After buying from me, people would realize that they could go ten or twenty minutes down the road and buy a house for about the same price, in a much nicer area that wasn't surrounded by refineries. This was a real problem. The people who were tied to my neighborhood were people that worked at these refineries or who had friends and family close by or who wanted to stay near the schools their kids were already growing up in, and they had roots there. This was when I came up with the idea of utilizing Facebook at the time, I didn't realize it would have as big an impact as it did. My logic was that people always post about life events, they share pictures when they find out they are having a baby, or pictures of when they get engaged or married. They share these important moments online and all their friends and family get excited. Some people do it with a new dog or a new car, so why not a new house?

I mean, why is that not just as exciting? I certainly think it is!

Now, let's say that somebody has 500 friends on Facebook, and you post a picture of them holding a "sold" sign on their timeline. That has the potential of 500 people now knowing that they bought a home from you. Let's say they have a real estate agent; if you tag the agent in that post, if the agent has maybe 1,000 friends. That's 1,500 people as well as an endorsement from an agent of your homes. That's free advertising!

So, I started doing that, and suddenly my cancelation rates when down. After a few months, I started wondering why. Then I realized when I do the post on my customers' timelines, all their friends and family are basically saying, "You made a good decision, I am happy for you." They click "like." The comments say: "Congratulations," "We're going to barbecue," or something similar. You see, when people make a major purchase they often go on a major roller coaster of emotions. These emotions range from the high excitement that they feel when they sign the paperwork, to the anxiety and fear they get when they start to look at mortgages and down payments. When I started posting on Facebook, the emotional roller coaster of "ups and downs" were for the most part canceled out by my clients' friends and family constantly reaffirming the decision they made as a good one. The emotional highs stayed high and the lows, along with a good portion of the worries and fears, dissipated. Then something else started happening, when I looked back at the older posts, I started to see names in the comments that I recognized. The names I was seeing were people that had come to visit the community or bought a home from me maybe a month later or even a year after the post. I'd have people come in the office and say "My friend is buying a home from you." I would say, "Oh! They told you about us!?" and they would say, "No, I saw it on their Facebook page."

I then decided to expand on my Facebook strategy, I started putting a picture of their home on their Facebook timeline every week to two, as an update of what's happening on their house as it progresses through the stages of construction. So, as it's being built, I'd do an update saying, "we broke ground — look!", or "Your foundation is poured — look!" or "Your home is being framed — look!" All of that is exciting, and their friends keep chiming in and reinforces the decision they made to buy. I went from a 20-30% cancellation rate to no cancellations for almost eight months straight. And my Facebook campaign was one of the only things I changed. On a side note, as I write this book, I am currently on a close to 3-year streak in my current community of zero cancellations by a customer after we have started construction of their home. It eventually also got to where probably 30-40% of my business was coming from that style of post. Not everybody is going to tell every single person they know the news in their life even if it's happy news. In fact, people are 10 times more likely to tell people about a negative experience than a positive one. And you being linked to their Facebook page means they are much less likely to voice their dissatisfaction with your homes and their experience with you, since they know you are watching.

All these positive results with Facebook caused me to look at other social media platforms or, at least, to experiment and see what results I could potentially generate. I found the information I could gather, the referrals I could get, the ways I could utilize this market. The fact is, with the content you put out there, all of your marketing streams intertwine and help promote each other. For example, when I'm sending out an email, it contains links below my signature to our community social media pages. And each one of those pages have links to each other.

When someone buys a home from me or simply just visits my community, I immediately send them a follow up email that includes a link to our YouTube videos. You want to give people all the content you can, so they can view and share it as many times as possible. You want to make sure all of your social media sites provide links to each other so there is a never-ending stream of information for anyone that is open to receiving it.

The social media platforms will use algorithms to determine what content is viewed more often and by who. The way they do this is by seeing how each of us respond to certain content. If you constantly comment, like or share a particular person's posts, their content will show up more often in your news feed. If you never interact with certain people, then it's much less likely you will see their posts in your news feed. Therefore, it is very important to try to get as many people to interact with your posts as possible, if you post something more people will see it. You always want your posts to be engaging, attractive and relevant. These algorithms affect you on a much broader level as well, the more interaction your posts have the more they will show up in searches for whatever they are relevant to. When you do a Google search for something the sites that have had the most interaction with that particular subject are the ones that rise to the top. Google assumes they are the most relevant and accurate because they are the most looked at.

One effective way to get people to engage with you online is to offer them something in exchange for their interaction with your content. I have seen car companies do giveaways for a free car to a random person that likes, comments and shares their content on Facebook. The people that interact with that content will start to see more from that page later and obviously sharing the post puts it in front of more people simultaneously. Obviously, giving a free car away is a bit extreme, but finding something that's appealing to people shouldn't be too hard. A gift card or maybe even a donation to the charity of their choice is simple and relatively inexpensive.

Now, let's look at each social media platform individually.

Facebook

To start off, for people who don't yet know much about Facebook, they may not realize that there are different types of Facebook "accounts" which I liken to being two sides of the same coin. Each has its own uses and is equally important to our SmackDown strategy.

Facebook account

You "Friend" people

You can post on the walls of your Facebook Friends.

You can tag Facebook Friends in pictures and posts.

People can't "Check In" or "Like" a personal account.

Typically for people, not businesses or places or events.

One is a personal account, which is what people normally have and use in everyday life. It's about you. This is where your friends and family are 'friends' with your account and where you post pictures of your car, what you had for dinner, your pets, your grandkids, etc.

The other kind of account is a business page or sometimes called a "fan page," which is specifically used for promotion or marketing/advertising. The business page is one that you can "like" and "check-in" at. Celebrities and businesses usually have a page that you can "like." My Facebook account is always named "Builder Name Community Name." Because Facebook wants an account to have a first and last name, as it is meant for a person not a business.

If your builder name or community name has more than one word in it then you should not have a space between them just like in the example I gave. Facebook will kick back the name if you try to have too many words in those fields. The reason for using this technique instead of your personal name is that your builder and community names have more recognition and clout than the name of an individual. If you are a real estate agent, then I would recommend putting your brokerage name with your name as your name is part of the brand you are building. For example, John Smith Generic Realty so that you can build a brand in your name and capitalize on the name recognition of your brokerage as well. Again, I stick to the one-word format, so Facebook is more likely to accept it as a first and last name. You can capitalize certain parts of it so that it's more recognizable as separate words like in the example above.

My business page is named something similar but since it's not required in a first and last name format I usually have it as "Builder Name @ Community Name."

At first it may be confusing remembering what each one does and what they are used for. So, an easy way to remember which one is which is:

Personal account – you "friend" and business page – you "like".

The Checklist

Now, let's dig a little deeper and talk about what each one does and how you can utilize them.

The personal account is mainly used to update clients and real estate agents with photos on the client's wall. The business page is the main platform used to actively advertise inventory, incentives and promotions. It is very important to note that Facebook does not want businesses to advertise with the personal account, they want all of that done through the Facebook business pages. This is the main reason you do not want to use the account to actively advertise, only to post photos on the walls of clients to update them in order to gain exposure to their friends and family. It is important to make sure both pages or "accounts" have content on them. If someone sees one of your posts and they click it, but your page is empty they are highly unlikely to contact you.

You obviously want to gain your client's' permission before posting anything on their Facebook walls. I haven't had any trouble doing this, as I always offer my clients an incentive in return. When someone writes a contract, I let them know that part of the incentive we have to offer them for buying the home is a social media incentive. We let our clients know that we typically spend, 1% of the price of the home on advertising. If they agree to help us advertise, we will slash 1% off the price. And all we ask are these three simple things at the time of contract: to add us on their personal page as a friend, "like" our business page and "check in" at our business on their timeline.

The total incentive I give varies from home to home, but I usually tie a small portion of whatever it is to the social media incentive. So maybe it could be 1% of the price of the house. If it's a $400,000 house, that's a $4,000 incentive. This sounds like a lot of money just to friend you and check-in on Facebook but that's what makes it easy for them to buy into it. Since it's a part of the incentive I would have already given them anyway, you aren't giving anything more than you normally would off the home price.

I ask people to fulfill the social media tasks at the contract signing, in order for the incentive to apply to the home. You don't want to wait, and hope people do it later, because they'll either forget or it just won't be as important to them since they already have the incentive and you will have lost your leverage. This is just my strategy, and you may find one that works better and is more effective for you, but I have had very few problems getting anyone that has a Facebook account to participate. How you present the opportunity is key to getting your clients to buy in. I've heard other people in the business say things like "can you friend us on Facebook, so I can put pictures on your wall every week?" I'm sorry but that just sounds weird and slightly creepy and is certainly not going to be an effective way to get clients to buy into the strategy.

Each of the following three steps are important in their own way.

1. Friending the account will link your client to the Facebook account that you will use to update them on the construction process of their new home.

2. Liking the business page will increase the number of likes your page has but will also link your client to your business page. This will allow your client to see any posts you make with your business page in the future thus creating an "organic" audience. An organic audience is an audience that will find you and your content without you having to pay for advertising.

3. And the check in on your client's timeline will raise the number of check in's you have on your business page. Also, since their check in will show up on their wall, the check-in will also serve as a "free" announcement to their social network that they are in your place of business, probably considering buying a home from you. Suddenly, their friends might ask, "Are you buying a house?" People will probably start congratulating your client, affirming their decision to

purchase a house from you while letting everyone know they bought a home from you!

These page likes and check-ins are also useful in another way. The ability to generate likes and comments provides something called "social proof." Social proof is the perception of how respected your product and or page is based on how many likes and check-in's it has. If you look at a page, let's say Disney World, you will see Disney has millions of likes and check in's. That's because people **enjoy** letting their friends know, "I'm at Disney World today." It's a happy and exciting statement, just how you want people to feel when they buy a house from you.

When I look at some of my competition's business pages, they have very few check-ins and "likes." Then I look at my page, and I've got thousands of likes... who would you rather go with? Someone who has generated so much enthusiasm that people have gone online and made the effort to "like" their page, or a competitor who seems to have no one ranting and raving about them. When people look at the two pages, they will wonder, "Why is this one more popular? Let's go see what the buzz is about." Social media platforms help companies and people build reputations. Likes and check in's also support your business in the algorithms we referenced earlier, which will help your content show up online more often to more people.

The most viral posts and pictures are going to be, usually, at the beginning and then the end of the process holding the "sold" sign in front of their lot or in front of their house that they just bought. You want to try to do something that's funny or eye-catching. We've had people jump up in the air, holding their keys in the picture. Or we created one photo where we put the "sold" sign over the real estate agent's face to be funny. The idea is to make a post fun and special to get people interested in seeing what the post is about.

It takes six months or more to build a home in my community, so we might have between twelve and twenty-four images posted over time on a buyer's Facebook page. I take one or two pictures of each house, usually once a week, and I upload them to an app called Dropbox into a folder I titled "Weekly." In the folder, I delete the photos from the previous week and add the new photos. Obviously, you'll want to keep this folder organized so you can keep track of which house belongs to who. You don't want to post the wrong home picture on someone's wall. After I upload the photos I will edit and crop them to make them as attractive as possible and simply post the photos on each customer's Facebook wall and write a simple sentence. "Look! Your house is being framed," or "You got a roof!" or "Walls are going up!" The sentence should identify what's happening but keep it short and simple. It usually takes about 30-45 min a week to do this effectively, a small amount of time for a strategy that has proven to be incredibly powerful in driving in new traffic.

How your photos look will have a big impact on how effective the posts are for you. If your pictures are of a messy home site or interior photos of a house with no lighting, you probably won't get much new traffic from that. You want to avoid any photos that are dark or blurry. I typically post one picture of the front of the exterior of the home. There's usually so much going on every week or so that the exterior changes as time progresses, and it's nice for people to see the gradual change.

Facebook Business Page

There is also a completely different side of Facebook that most people know nothing about. Though the business page isn't entirely free, there are options that are very inexpensive and very effective. Through your business page, you can pay Facebook to advertise for you using "ad campaigns". You do need to be aware that you will need to create your business page first to do this. There should be several links on the Facebook homepage that say, "create business or fan page," one of which is at the bottom of the main login page at Facebook.com

The Checklist

Facebook currently has approximately fifteen different paid advertising campaigns, which allow you to target very different demographics as well as accomplish various goals with your advertising.

- Boost your posts
- Promote your Page
- Send people to your website
- Increase conversions on your website
- Get installs of your app
- Increase engagement in your app
- Reach people near your business
- Raise attendance at your event
- Get people to claim your offer
- Get video views
- Collect leads for your business

I've mainly used two forms of ads on Facebook. One is a **"like campaign"** or **"promote page,"** which I utilize when I'm trying to generate "likes" for my business page. And as we discussed earlier, likes can be very useful to you.

To use **Promote Page** to get likes, you click on the "promote" button, which you will see on your business page. It's blue with white text, on the top right, and it's easy to see. Or you can go to the Facebook drop down menu on the top right of the screen and click "create ad." After clicking the "create ad" button, Facebook will ask you numerous straightforward and easy to answer questions such as, "How much money do you want to spend?" and "Who do you want to see it?"

These questions refer to demographics and you can set who you want the ads to target, in reference to age or gender. There are many ways to define your audience when using the campaigns. You can narrow where they are seen by selecting specific cities, states or even countries. You can also narrow down by interest. By doing this you are putting your advertisement in front of people that have searched for those specified interests. It is very important to note that the more defined your audience, the higher the campaign cost will be.

The Checklist

My main goal, when I first created my page, was to establish my social proof. So, I just focused on increasing "likes" in general. I did this in a few different ways. One way was to invite all the people I was friends with on my normal Facebook account to like my new business page. You can do this by going to your business page itself. Right under your cover photo, there will be a small tab that says "more" with a downward arrow. After you select that tab, an option that says, "invite friends", will appear. If you click on the option, you will be able to invite anyone that is friends with your personal account page to like your Facebook business page. You can invite the friends of any account that is linked to that business page.

Another way I increase likes is to promote my page through paid Facebook advertising campaigns. Since my goal first and foremost is to add likes in general, I am not too picky about who likes the page and where they live. When I set up the campaign, I specified no particular age, all genders and all locations for the audience selections. I made my target demographic as broad as possible. The broader the settings when you pick your audience, the less the likes cost you. I was able to significantly increase my page likes for very little money.

Obviously before resorting to paid advertising to add likes, you want to add some content to the page. You should add high quality virtual tours and photos of your homes and community and its amenities, before perusing this strategy. An empty business page gives people no reason to click the like button and follow it. High quality content will make it extremely likely that anyone that sees your page will like it and possibly want to learn more about what you have to offer.

When I started my business page my Facebook budget was $100 a month, and I was spending three-quarters of that for "likes" in the beginning. We went from almost none to over a thousand likes in a few months. It was a huge difference for very little cost.

Once you have a decent number of likes established, you want to start to focus more on WHO is liking your page. You want your likes to be more focused and targeted to the people who are most likely to buy your homes. Remember though, since your advertising audience is now more focused you will get less likes for your money, so don't be discouraged when you see less of a result. Since the people that have liked your page will likely see your future posts, it's beneficial for your audience to be local and interested in buying a home. This will mean they are more likely to visit you than someone who lives thousands of miles away and may not even have an interest in buying a home. Once you have your location, demographic and keywords set, you hit "go," and now what's going to happen is instead of getting maybe a thousand "likes" for a hundred bucks, you're going to get maybe a hundred "likes" for a hundred bucks. But don't worry! These refined likes are going to be far more relevant because the likes are real people who are actively engaging with your product. And now, when you're posting about something for free and not engaging in paid advertisements, you've created an organic following that's free.

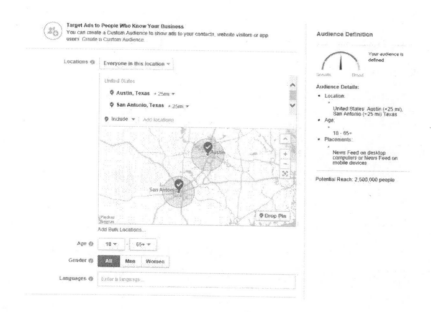

Once I start an ad that seems to generate a positive response, I let it run continuously, using the same three-quarters of my Facebook budget. I employed this strategy for around six months in total, during the first three months, I focused on building as many "likes" as possible; and in the second three months, I changed the targeted audience to generate defined "likes".

A "**Boosted Post**" is the second type of advertising campaign I have used. A Boosted Post lets you set up certain criteria for your post audience and keeps your post in their news feeds longer, for better exposure. You can advertise anything, from an inventory home to a huge sale. You can set your target audience to reside within a certain mile radius of "this" city, with "this" age. The Boosted Post will attract people who have searched "similar topics" through keywords or "interests" as Facebook likes to call them. So, I could set my target age demographic from 35-55 or 25-55. I also select "men" or "women" who have liked other pages or topics related to the keywords we specify, such as "real estate". You can also input the names of other larger builders in your area, and the larger brokerages of real estate in your area as keywords in the interest category. By doing this, you capitalize on their marketing and brand recognition. Now that you've inputted these big companies in your desired keyword search, anyone who has searched for those "interests" is more likely to see your ad! I also recently figured out how to gain likes from the boosted posts to make them even more effective. To view the results for any of your advertising on Facebook, click on a tab labeled "insights." Once you are on the insights page you can click to see who has liked your boosted post and off to the side of their name is a little link to invite them to like your page. Inviting people to like your page helps to make sure they will see your future posts by adding them to your organic audience. Now you're getting even more benefit from the boosted posts!

Most people use the "create ad" option to create a post to advertise with. I do not. I post my advertisement on my timeline first instead. I leave the post there for a day or two and then come back to it later to boost it by simply going back to the post and clicking "boost post" There are two main reasons I do it this way; first, I want my "organic audience" to see my posts so that I get exposure without spending money. These are all the people that have liked and followed your page already, you shouldn't have to pay for them to see it. For this reason, I also specify when I am setting up my audience parameters that exclude anyone that has liked my page from seeing the ad. You can select this under an option called "excluded connections."

The second reason I do not use the ad creator is that I want that post to be content for later visitors to my page to see. If you create an ad with Facebook's ad creator, it will not show up on your page when people visit your page.

I mentioned earlier about using three quarters of my Facebook budget on gaining "likes" for the first six months, the other quarter of the budget in the beginning was used to experiment with boosted posts. After the six months were up, I flipped that ratio to three quarters for boosted posts and one quarter for page likes. I felt I had a good number of total likes, but I wanted to continue to add a small number of new likes each month.

What you're going to see is the longer you run boosted ads and the more money you allocate towards the campaign; the more people will look at your posts and the more people will find you. Facebook has analytics that will tell you, "This many people clicked on your photos," "This many people "liked" your post," "This many people commented on your post," and "This many people shared it."

It's important to note that while previously the boosted posts were only one-quarter of my budget, I was using that time to experiment and figure out which posts generated the best response because every industry has its own quirks. Depending on the product you're selling, people respond to ads differently. I noticed that when I posted information about an inventory home, with pictures of a finished home, people responded to it more. The audience who responded consisted primarily of people who were actively looking for a home, and who wanted a home right then. When I offered "This is a lot for sale" or "Look at our community amenities," the ad didn't get anywhere near as much response as a finished home did. The finished home received twice as much of a response, compared to everything else.

In the majority of my boosted posts, I have seen people tag their significant others and write, "Honey, look at this." Or people might ask me, "What's the address of this house?" or, "Is this on MLS?" I had a real estate agent just the other day ask me, "What's the price of this house? I may have a client for your community, please call me." If it's an unsuccessful post, it may only have a few

likes after a day or two. This is where you learn from your mistakes and start over with a new post. My experience has been that boosted posts with videos in them perform the worst. I think this is because most people look at your ads on a mobile device, and it just takes too long to watch an entire video. I am still experimenting though to see if I can make the videos more effective. Still photos are easy and instant, and your audience can scroll through them quickly.

Many people may see $100 a month as a lot of money, especially if they're just starting out. But, if you follow what we're saying here, the payback should be tenfold. And the cool thing is you can see the actual real time results when you view the analytics. Facebook provides data and graphs that show you how long the post has been up and how many likes it has generated.

If your post received no clicks or only a few, you might say "All right, I'm just going to stop this one." If it's got a hundred clicks, you might say, "Well, I'm going to add to that budget," because you can change the budget as you go. It's really important to know that you don't have to start off with $100.00, you can start off with as little as one dollar per day. For $5.00, the price of a coffee at a Starbucks, you can do this and start experimenting. As you gain confidence, you can scale into bigger and bigger budgets.

So again, the strategy is:

1.) Promote the page to get page likes with three quarters of the budget and experiment with boosted posts with one quarter of the budget for 6 months.

Phase 1: Get "likes" from anywhere (first 3 months)

Phase two: Get "targeted likes" to your location (3-6 months in and ongoing)

2.) After 6 months, flip the budget so the boosted posts are using the majority of the budget. Again, I believe posts featuring finished inventory homes are the most impactful, but you can post about whatever you feel is the most exciting and engaging topics you have to offer.

I highly recommend that after reading this section once, you go to your computer and open Facebook, reread this section, and follow this process step by step. The only way to learn is by doing.

Facebook Listings

I have started doing something new recently, and though it has only been a few weeks it looks fairly effective. I created a cross between an MLS listing and a social media blog along with creating by Facebook business page for each one of my inventory homes. That means each home has its very own Facebook page. That entire page is strictly posts, videos, pictures etc., about that one home.

A lot of the things I do may or may not be as effective for people that work in other areas of real estate besides new home sales, but I think this is something that would be extremely effective for real estate agents as they could do this for each one of their listings. The name of the inventory home's business page is its address, that way people know it's a home that is for sale and its location. For example, 123 Sherman Drive, would be the format I would use. You would set up this page the same way you set up your business page. Make sure to add content like photos and videos before you start posting and boosting posts.

One thing to note, the boosts you do with this page may not perform as well as the boosts you do with your community page. A Builder or brokerage name will give your main business pages advertising a bit of recognition. But, the inventory homes page will be more targeted, and you can send people directly to them through your other pages and marketing efforts.

This page can also be used as part of your follow up. If you have a real estate agent call or a prospect come by, you can send the prospective client a follow up email with a link to each of your inventory pages. It's almost like you have a website for each of your homes without you having to actually design one! Links to the Facebook page can also be put into MLS notes or put on other social media pages, all with the intent to drive traffic to a more focused presentation.

You will also want to make sure to delete the business page once you have sold that home. You don't want someone showing up at a new home owner's house trying to get in to see the home because they think it's for sale.

Emerging Technologies on Facebook

There are some new and interesting features I've recently started experimenting with on Facebook. The first of which is Facebook Live. You now have the ability to live stream on Facebook so that people can view you or whatever you are filming live, as if they are watching you on TV. They even have drones now that can stream with the Facebook Live feature. I have been experimenting with this in ways such as inventory home tours where you can share video while on a live stream where people can interact by asking questions while watching. My co-worker and I even did a live stream while flying a drone around an inventory home as she fielded questions from our live audience. After you finish creating a live video, the video stays in your news feed as a normal video so people can watch it later as well. Currently this can be done with both your Facebook "account" and "business page."

The other new technology that Facebook, as well as a few

other social media platforms have started taking advantage of is the development of "360 cameras." These allow you to shoot still photos or live video, and for your audience to have the ability to pan around and look at various things that the camera records 360 degrees around the entire area. These cameras have been around for a little while, and they are getting cheaper and more advanced which allows more people to take advantage of the technology. Imagine using this with a Virtual Reality headset and being able to show someone what a home looks like without having to leave your office. You can show them homes that are across the globe or in the case of new home builders, homes that aren't even built yet. When you take advantage of new cutting-edge technology, you will create an experience for your customers that they will not find anywhere else and one that they are likely to remember.

YouTube

When somebody wants to learn a new skill or how to do something, they now turn to YouTube. Anything you could want to know; how to cook something, how to fix something, it's all on YouTube. And YouTube is growing at 40% year on year and 60% in mobile.

YouTube is the one social media platform that most people in real estate don't take advantage of enough. Using YouTube has allowed me to effectively showcase my community, floor plans and home sites in a way that no other platform could.

I first started using YouTube a couple years ago by uploading a few videos of some of the floor plans I built in my community. These videos were of plans that I couldn't always show people in person because we didn't have models of them. So, once I had a finished home of a certain plan I would video the home and add it to my library of videos. Eventually, we also added these videos to our webpage so that people visiting the page would be able to watch to get a better idea of what the plan was like. Seeing a video provides a three-dimensional view, does much more for your buyer than a floor plan brochure or plain photos.

I honestly never knew the amount of traffic our website got, particularly the page for my community. Shortly after we added the YouTube videos to the website, I looked at my analytics on YouTube and there was a huge spike on the day the videos were added. That basically told me that people are looking, and when they saw the videos, they all started clicking on them.

People like video because it's engaging. They don't have to figure out what a plan looks like, they can see it. It's the next best thing to being there. A lot of people will look at a floor plan and its just lines on a piece of paper to them. The video gives them the information they need to form an opinion and make a decision when they normally would not have been able to do so.

The more content and engaging information you can send to your clients, the more engaged they will become. And the more time they invested in you, the less time will be left over for your competition.

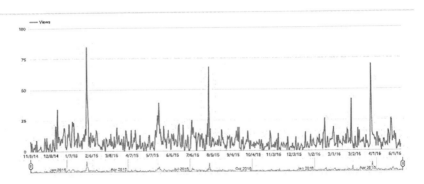

When used in conjunction with the other SmackDown strategies, YouTube becomes even more effective. For example, when I use my follow up email system "Constant Contact" I almost always include links to appealing and relevant YouTube videos. Or when I send out a follow-up email to a prospective customer, I always include links to videos of my floor plans or drone videos showcasing my community and its amenities. If you have an out of town buyer, every other builder or agent they talk to probably just sends over a few pictures. If in contrast you send over photos, video walkthroughs, community videos and whatever else you might have up your sleeve, you will likely stand out and you will capture the buyer as a prospect and a customer easily.

I currently sell in an acreage community in the Texas Hill Country, surrounded by rolling hills, covered in trees, with rivers winding through canyons and well...you get the idea. It's an amazing place and video is the perfect way to show people its beauty. When I first arrived at this community, I hired a retired military drone pilot to fly a drone over the neighborhood. Using the drone, he videoed the gated and guarded entrance and showcased the amenities in the community, such as the pool, the playground, the tennis court and basketball court. The success of this video motivated me to purchase my own drone. I have used the drone to video homes, community amenities and even live stream while flying! All this content is put on each of my social media accounts and is included in the follow up emails I send out via links to videos on YouTube. That content is given out everywhere it possibly can be so that prospective buyers can see it and share it. By linking each platform together as well as including links in your emails, you can generate traffic from and to all of your social media sites and websites. Creating a web of information for your customers to play around in, the more time they will spend in your web and the less likely they will end up finding your competition. My basic plan of action with YouTube is to upload videos of my community, each of my available floor plans and the lots I have to build on. Once I accomplished this, I sent out the links to them in my follow up emails and posted them on Facebook. If you are a real estate agent, you should upload videos of your listings and even make little video blogs highlighting what you do that's different from other agents. Adding videos like this will help show people how you set yourself apart from the competition.

Don't ever be afraid to experiment and make your own videos. You will never learn to do anything new unless you try something you've never done!

Other Social Media Platforms

Here is a list of the top 10 social media platforms, ranked by estimated unique monthly visitors:

1 – **Facebook** – 1,100,000,000 Monthly Visitors

2 – **YouTube** – 1,000,000,000 Monthly Visitors

3 – **Twitter** – 310,000,000 Monthly Visitors

4 – **LinkedIn** – 255,000,000 Monthly Visitors

5 – **Pinterest** – 250,000,000 Monthly Visitors

6 – **Google Plus** – 120,000,000 Monthly Visitors

7 – **Tumblr** – 110,000,000 Monthly Visitors

8 – **Instagram** – 100,000,000 Monthly Visitors

9 – **Reddit** – 85,000,000 Monthly Visitors

10 – **VK** – 80,000,000 Monthly Visitors

Please remember this list is the social media landscape as this book is being written (2018) and things can change in an instant. We all remember Myspace, don't we? It is also important to point out that just because one platform is ranked higher than another, doesn't mean it is more effective for you to use.

It is my opinion, at this moment in time, Instagram is much more effective for selling homes than Twitter or LinkedIn. I've found the clear majority of people, at least currently, who are on Instagram are typically younger (teens to late 20s). To me, Instagram's current format and demographic isn't as effective for the audience I'm generating with Facebook. Let's face it, teenagers are not buying homes, at least not yet anyway. But that still doesn't mean that I won't use Instagram at all and I will continue to keep my ears to the ground in the case that Instagram adapts to better support the real estate market. In fact, since Facebook purchased Instagram I have already started to see more of a push to advertise on Instagram using Facebook Ads. In the small amount of time since they have added this feature I have not yet seen much of a return from any of the advertising I have done on Instagram. Instagram seems to get more clicks and likes but not much as far as real buyers wanting to come see you.

We've used Pinterest to get our name out, and to get followers. In my opinion Pinterest is more for brand recognition, but using it is free and takes almost no time so it's always worth a few minutes a week. You can post an amazing picture of one of your most luxurious bathrooms, and if the name of your Pinterest account is "Your Builder at Your Neighborhood," that's a bit of advertising right there. People from all over the world will follow you, so it's not very location specific, and some of the people following you may not be anywhere near the location you're selling in, but your name is getting out there and chances are, it will eventually get to somebody in your area. I make it a point once a week to just put a new image on Pinterest, and people will follow. Often, it's people from our Facebook page who will follow, because Facebook suggests some of those links. Pinterest has not generated the impact Facebook or YouTube has had, but it's not a platform to ignore either. My opinion of Twitter is that it is similar to going to a hilltop and just yelling random stuff: you don't know who's listening to you. It works better for celebrities and major announcements or if you have a lot of people following and you're a nationwide company. I have not done much with it at all, so far. The people who follow you are so random and so undefined in interests and location that it would be hard to use this in a very effective way since my promotion activity has to be location specific. Again, that does not mean I will not continue to try new things and see if I can figure an effective way of using it, I just do not see one at the present time.

Social Media in Summary

How important has social media been to my $10 million-dollar six-month conversion?

I think it's the platform which, along with my follow-up

makes up probably the two most important strategies I've employed. If I don't have the platform to tell people what I have to offer, they won't ever walk into my office.

Social media is getting more important, especially with the younger millennial population. If you're not including social media as part of your overall marketing strategy you're not in the game and the longer you wait to start, the further behind you will be.

V. Info Tubes

Info Tubes are a way you can use flyers to get customers into your office.

Let's say you're in a neighborhood where the location of another builder's model, or open house, has a bit of an advantage over yours. Maybe there's a big-name builder with a huge marketing machine there, or maybe you're in there with a few builders with big name recognition. They probably get a lot of traffic just from their name and from the marketing they do. They also probably have a good number of real estate agents that bring people specifically to them and nobody else. A lot of the people that come through a neighborhood to see that builder might drive through the neighborhood looking at a couple of their homes. Or maybe someone has come to your community to see a resale home they found on a listing. If they see an info tube, it's a non-threatening way for them to get information from you.

Physically, an info-tube is a little box or tube that you can put flyers in. It may be attached to or next to your "Sold" or "Available" signs. If the potential customers visit your community and doesn't have a lot of time to house shop or aren't into being pestered by a salesperson, they will most likely not visit your model home. But, as they drive through the neighborhood, they  are likely to pull out one of those flyers from the info tubes you've set up.

I always put info tubes on sold homes as well as available homes because every sold home is like a mini-model home and can and should be used to help you sell more homes. When you're driving through my neighborhood, I post flyers that will let prospective clients know they are welcome to look at a particular home and that there are other homes we have in the community, and that I can build the homes they look at on different lots if they like.

With any luck, the eye candy that's on the flyer or in the home will make them want to come and see you in person. Just remember, do not give them too much information. I always leave the price off the info tube flyers so prospective buyers still must contact you for more information.

Flyers and Postcards

I've used flyers in a couple of different ways in my neighborhood. Currently I'm in a neighborhood with five or six different builders. With that in mind I've created what I call a **parade of homes flyer**. It's like a scavenger hunt. The front of it has a picture of three or four homes with the description next to it. On the back it has a map enabling you to see where each of my inventory homes is located. Make sure to also mark all your sold homes on the map as well, this will do wonders for generating urgency if the map shows that a lot has sold and not much is left. After visiting each of these the customers feel like they have seen what the community has to offer so a good number of people never even look at the other builders. Remember, the more time the buyers spend with you, the less they will spend with your competition.

The information I put on the flyer is more basic information and bullet points of the strengths of the home or homesite, like square footage and number of bedrooms. Let's say this home is going to have a huge back patio. This is the eye candy, the strength of the home, things like this need to be on the flyer in picture and description. You only have a few seconds or less to capture somebody's attention, so you list those stand-out features with some creative description and have a few pictures of the home. To me, a picture of a half-finished home is not appealing. So if the home isn't finished you can have a picture of a house that's the same floor plan, or a similar floor plan, but finished. You could put a little note that says, "Picture is a representation only." People will understand that. The main idea is to capture their attention with the little time that you have, in the little space you have on that flyer.

Every flyer needs a call to action and it needs to be quick and easy. It should just let them know if they ever need help with anything, or want to tour one of the homes, or have questions or anything, they can contact you. I usually tell them, on the flyers, that they can email, text or call, because everybody has a different comfort level.

Letting your potential customers choose how to contact you allows them to feel the most comfortable with their interaction with you, which is what you want, so that they will in fact engage with you. For example, unless I'm 100% interested, I'd rather just shoot off an email or a text and get the information I need to make my own decision. I do not want to be sold something and I think a good amount of people feel the same way.

Apart from using info tubes with the flyers, I also drop flyers off at real estate agent offices. I do this so that they always have something with our info on it, again if you're out of sight you're out of mind. You would want to include flyers for floor plans that can be built, standard features and inventory homes that you may have. On these flyers I always include the pricing, the agents would not want to waste their time coming to see you or having to call you to find out if the home you have is even in their client's price range.

VI. The Community/In Home Experience

The community and in-home experience is the experience that people will expect to have each time they come to your model home or to your community.

Feelings

To describe the community and in-home experience in one word, I'd say "Feelings."

A person who has been very influential to me has always said, **"People might not remember what you say to them, or what you do, but they will ALWAYS remember the way you make them feel."** If you make a prospective client comfortable, or feel like a part of the family, then they're going to remember that.

Winston Churchill's mother once spoke about her dining experiences with two British politicians. She said after dining with one she left thinking that he was the most interesting man she had ever met. And after dining with the other she left thinking that SHE was the most interesting person HE had ever met. He had spent the whole night talking about her and making her feel important instead of talking about himself the entire time. Obviously, that was a better dinner than the other.

People who sell Mary Kay cosmetics are often taught in their initial training to pretend their customers have a sign around their necks that say, "treat me like I am the most interesting and important person in the world." People just want to feel happy and important. Doing things to make that them feel important before and after the sale is an easy way to get referrals down the road.

Where I work, our buyers have numerous walk-throughs of their home during various stages of the build. Recently I have started doing something new: during the framing of the home I will write little messages on the framing of their home. When they come to do the frame walk they see the little messages and they have always reacted positively and a lot of times have taken pictures of them and shared them on their social media accounts. If you know your buyers are religious, you could write a little scripture or something for them or just a couple of little notes here and there. These things are easy and take almost no time at all but could mean the world to your buyers. Another part of the experience is making sure the potential buyer doesn't feel too pressured; they don't feel as if they are in a used car dealership. Now, that does not mean there is no pressure whatsoever. You should always give them a reason to buy sooner than later but they should never feel like you care more about the sale than you care about them.

That's the way I operate my model. I usually tell them these exact things, "It's different here. You should feel the difference in the way we treat you. You should see the difference in the way we operate. It should be a totally different experience. A better experience."

For example, if you come in my model on a weekend, we have sports games on the TV. We have a refrigerator full of water, soft drinks, kids' drinks, and beer and wine. I have home owners that will come and sit down in front of the TV if there's a football game on, pop open a beer, watch the game, and just talk. A lot of the times they've already bought their home, so there's no reason other than to just come and hang out. It's because of the fact that we've let them know they're welcome here. It's not a sales office, it's our home. It's a representation of what we want to offer somebody. This different experience makes the time spent with our clients more memorable.

Another part of my in-home experience is constantly trying to have a stimulus for all five senses. The more you can implement this, the more memory triggers there are going to be.

You can stimulate smell by having plug-ins or cookies baking in the model.

You can trigger taste by having snacks, candy or drinks.

You have noise when you're coming into the model, from music or a game on TV.

There's the sight of the model home.

There's the tactile experience of the furnishings and finishes.

The more you're able to trigger all these senses, the more they're going to remember the experience in the model home. All these sensory experiences can generate memory and recall. Even schools have figured this out. When my son was studying for his fifth-grade statewide test, the teachers had the kids chew a certain flavor of gum while they studied. When they took the test, they gave them the same gum. The taste triggers memory; it allows you to recall something more easily. That's the way the human mind is wired. It's associative. So, if you can create associations, then you're building those memories. That's the effect we want to create.

In the end, the more of you they remember and the less of your competition, the better position you are in with each buyer that visits your community.

Events

Events are also part of the experience.

For example, I like to throw a "welcome party" for the newest homeowners in my community. Every 5 or 10 closings we will throw a party with the newest homeowners as the guests of honor. We invite everyone, even the other builders' home owners. This helps to demonstrate the way we treat our customers. We include them.

We had a party in my last community about two and a half years ago. Almost all of our home owners came, and the ones that bought from the other builder showed up. The most common response that I got to the party was, "Wow, this is awesome. Thank you for doing this. My own builder didn't even do this for us."

We also have little giveaways for the kids and home owners. We even found an easy way to turn it into a marketing event. I let people know that if you check in on our community page with

Facebook the moment you walk in the door, you will receive an entry into our giveaway

Let's say you had 30 people show up. Those 30 people all have at least a couple hundred friends each, probably many more than that. That's a lot of people seeing those check-ins on Facebook. So, even if they bought from another builder, now suddenly, you've got the other builder's home owners tagging you on stuff and including you. In a way, they're almost endorsing you.

It's not just a marketing exercise though. We consider our home owners part of our family. That's part of the difference in the way we operate. It's not just, "We sold you a home, see you later." In my opinion, the sale doesn't end when they sign the contract or even when they get their keys. It's part of the whole SmackDown circle of service, coming back around for the referrals after the sale, or for when they buy their next house.

Going back to the basics, your neighborhood and your model need to look good. You need to have "Sold" signs up, and you need to have "Available" signs up. People need to know you're in the community. If your signs and model home are trashy, people expect your homes to be trashy. Perception is reality. The experience they have in your model and community will be the lasting impression they have about you.

In my neighborhood I have a strategy for which home sites I try to sell first. I usually set it up so that the homes closest to my model home are the ones I try sell first. That way later when you're driving through the neighborhood and you come to my model, and you're surrounded by "Sold" signs. The perception is, everything is sold.

All my available homes and lots are on the opposite side of the neighborhood, so that you don't see as many "Available" signs as you do "Sold" signs. You must drive through all those "Sold" signs to get to the "Available" signs. The perception is, "Oh my-gosh all these lots are sold, I need to act quickly if I want one." Some people put fake "Sold" signs up. I've never had to do that. There are builders out there who will put ten fake "Sold" signs up, so it doesn't look like everything's available, and that nobody's actually buying their product. Ask yourself, what if someone driving through the community only liked one lot and that lot said sold on it, but it really was not sold, and they left. They may have bought it!

VII. Apartment Trade Outs and Business Trade Outs

Sometimes you have two people that both have separate needs. These might be two businesses that both have a need for traffic or for customers. Why not capitalize on the fact that you can help each other?

Apartment Trade Outs

Let's say that there are people that have lived in an apartment complex close to your model home for a year or two. They probably chose that particular apartment complex because it's close to where they work, or where their family lives. They're probably already open to the idea of living in the area where you're building your homes.

The people already living in that area most likely want to stay nearby, but not everybody wants to live in an apartment forever. Most people do aspire to own a home at some point. It's part of that "American dream" right? Why not make it easier? Why not make it so you can supply them with some customers and they can supply you with some customers?

With this in mind, I approached a couple of apartment complexes owned by the same management company. I let them know we wanted to establish an equity program that could be promoted by them as a benefit of living there. For every year that people lived there, they got credit with us for a certain amount of equity in a new home. Each year (capped at 3) would equate to a certain amount of equity, meaning a small extra discount on a new home with us.

The management companies advertised with their new and current homeowners about this program. In turn, we sent them customers. Why would we send them people you ask? Well, if my customers have to wait six to nine months on average to build a home for them, they might need somewhere to live while it's being built, especially if they have already sold their previous home. Most apartment complexes are very strict on the terms of their leases, most don't like leases less than a year, much less six months or less, so they gave my customers a discounted rate, and they were more flexible on the lease terms. That meant that when my clients would say, "I've sold my house and I've got three months until my house is ready. Where could I get a short-term rental?" I'd send the client on to that apartment complex. It helps the customer and us, and it keeps their apartments full. They may end up losing a couple of customers to us because of the fact that we have this equity program, but they also gain customers by the fact that we're keeping a high turnover. They could lock in an apartment for three months and have three months to get somebody else in that apartment, rather than having it stay empty.

Does this work? Well, I was able to identify two people who lived at the apartment complexes who ended up coming in to my homes. One of those people was completely unaware that there was a program. They rented from the apartment complex before this program was in place and it wasn't part of their welcome packet. I let them know that this program was there which helped my buyer make the decision to buy. Now, if you're getting something free at one place, and you go to the competition and you're not getting the same deal, there's a perception we're giving you more. If we can get anything that's an edge, a unique proposition, then we win. How much traffic you get from this technique depends on how active and proactive, and how big the apartment complexes are, and how many of them there are. I didn't have a lot of apartment complexes around me, so it wasn't something that would have generated a ton of traffic. But if you're surrounded by at least a few apartment complexes, this could be very much worth a try.

Business Trade Outs

In addition, you want to be aware of any places that would be willing to refer you or have your cards or flyers. Let's say there's a local gym. A lot of people just moving into the area get established by signing up for a gym membership somewhere. Maybe they mention to the membership sales person that they're just moving into an apartment and looking for a home. If you already have a relationship with them it's more likely that you're going to get referred to the newcomer.

You should also try to think of every organization you already do business with in your personal life as well as your professional life. There are places like dry cleaners and restaurants that will let you put your business cards on a little wall or bulletin board for their customers to see. This may not get you a ton of traffic, but every little bit helps and adds up

VIII. Follow-Up

I tackle follow-up a little bit differently than most people. I am not the type who is going to bombard you with phone calls. I have too many prospects and customers who want to talk to me to be able to do that. But don't take that to mean I do not follow up. I am just selective on which buyers I spend the majority of my time working with. Depending on how much of a response I get, it may be more or less than with some other people.

If you walk into my model home, my goal is for you to leave me your contact info but especially your email address. I have several pre-templated emails I have saved on my computers desktop. When you leave, I click them, they pop up, I put your email address in there, possibly attach a few photos of plans I think you'd like, hit send, and boom, it's already in your box before you even get to the car. These emails have pictures of the potential buyer's favorite floor plans and/or links to videos of the community and plans. Something to keep them remembering what they saw there with you and the fact you sent it to them within minutes of them leaving you is usually a little impressive as well.

Why do I do this? Well, there's something that I call "getting house drunk." They look at ten houses from ten different builders or more! After they look at that many they all start to blur together in their memory, so they have no clue which one had what, and they don't remember much. I hope they remember a little bit more of us because of the experience they had in our model. Still, I'm going to send them videos, links, and pictures in this email. I'm going to send them content that they can share with other people. I'm going to send them all kinds of things and hope to get a response from them. If they remember any builder, it's going to be us.

I do it immediately because they're excited about buying the home, and that's why they're looking right now. They may not be excited a week from now, or two weeks from now, or when they've seen ten other homes. If you are not following up, if your name's not on their caller ID or in their email inbox, they will forget you. Out of sight, out of mind.

Constant Contact

Another program I put their email address into is called Constant Contact, which is a program I use for my follow up.

Constant Contact has had one of the biggest impacts in my business and it has been constant, no matter the demographic.

Let me say that again....

Constant Contact has had one of the biggest impacts in my business and it has been constant, no matter the demographic.

When I first moved into my current community, it was stagnant; it wasn't getting a lot of traction. So, we devised a plan to bring new floor plans into the neighborhood, an entire new series of homes. But how are people going to know we have this new amazing floor plans? If they don't know about it, it doesn't exist.

I got the word out through Constant Contact, through word-of-mouth, and through visiting real estate offices. I used social media and every other tool I had at my disposal. The whole SmackDown list was my way of getting the information out so as many people as possible knew we had this different product.

I can literally go back through the Constant Contact emails now and probably pinpoint at least five or six names on that first email we sent out that have all bought homes from us.

Social media, the other big-impact player, can be a little bit less or more effective, depending on the demographic. But Constant Contact is something that has been across-the-board always effective, no matter what price range I'm selling, no matter what area I am in. Whether it's Houston or San Antonio, whether it's in the Hill Country, or whether it's by refineries, this is the one constant that's always been there for me. Everyone uses email.

Constant Contact is not free. The cost depends on how many contacts you have in there. I have around 3,000 right now, which costs $40 - $60 a month. I've got dozens and dozens of sales from Constant Contact. The sale of one house will pay for that software for probably the remainder of your career. It's not expensive.

I send a Constant Contact email probably every two to three weeks. I don't believe in emailing people every day, or even every week. That will get you added to spam folders and a lot of people unsubscribe from your mailing list if you just constantly badger them. Nobody wants to be bothered. So, every two or three weeks I send out a mass email to thousands of email addresses I've accumulated over time, whether they're real estate agents, whether they're previous homeowners, or potential buyers. With

Constant Contact you can put them in different folders so that they only get the emails you want them to.

You can't just send out an email and expect a miracle; what you put in the email is equally important; your "content." You need to pay attention to what you're saying, who you're saying it to, and how often you're saying it. One reason I like Constant Contact is because I can see the results of each individual email I send out I see how many people have opened it. I see what links they've clicked on inside and how many times they've opened it. I see what time they opened it, and if they share it with somebody else. Constant Contact supplies a ton of analytics. The data will help you nail down what works and what doesn't work.

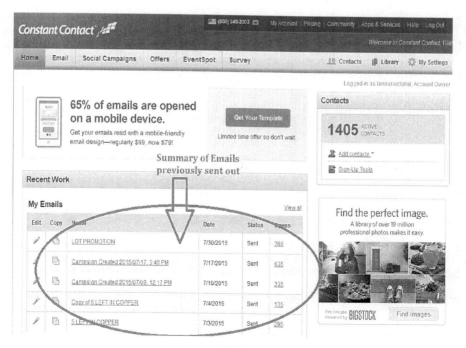

Effective Emails

Effective emails always include two important things.

The first thing to be aware of is the title of the email. If you don't have an interesting title, people won't open your email to begin with. Titles that work usually mention something about a "free" item. For example, "Free Metal Roof." Who wouldn't want to click on that? Usually a very direct message such as "Buy a house, get a pool" works. "Free three-car garages," or "Free four-car garages," often work. These are very direct and they're strengths you're communicating. I think this is where most marketing fails, people just think because you have a billboard or some other form of advertising with your name on it that it will motivate people to buy something. YOU NEED A MESSAGE! When you try to come up with your marketing message, imagine you have five to ten seconds to convince me as to why I should buy something from you.....GO!

One time I titled an email, "I regret to inform you..." the purpose of the email was to talk about a price increase that we were about to take. That one got a lot of opens, so the right title can get an email opened. The body of the email has more influence on whether they're going to respond to you or not and how they are going to respond. I didn't get a lot of feedback from that email, though everyone opened it to see what it was. I also got a higher amount of unsubscribes from that email. I think there were a lot of people still receiving my emails that weren't interested anymore and they hit Unsubscribe because the price change didn't affect them. Those people probably only opened the email because of the title being different and somewhat concerning than most other email titles.

The other thing to keep in mind is the body of the email. It needs to have appealing photos and or video. It needs to look professional. And most importantly it needs to have a message and a call to action. Don't just send out an email saying, "Happy Easter." If they have opened your email and are reading it, you have a captive audience for that moment and you should take full advantage of it.

I usually have a few topics in each email I send out, the incentive that we may have or our "Inventory of the Week," or "Inventory of the Month," and then another header that might talk about the lots we have left. This way you target different people who might be looking for different things. If somebody's looking to build from scratch and you're just talking about inventory homes or vice versa, it's not helpful. In my experience, people have always responded to finished inventory homes; I try to always include them in every email.

Each email sent should be treated like an experiment, varying content and headers and using analytics to discover which ones work best. There are a lot of different mindsets on follow-up. Some people prefer what are called drip campaigns, where it's a pre-templated series of emails. In my opinion, that works better for people that you just want to remain in contact with over a long period of time, like people that have already bought from you. It's not very dynamic to get people off the fence and into your model home. You can't pre-template an email for three months from now if you don't know what you're selling three months from now, and you don't know what your situation is.

I prefer to push out real-time on-the-ground information in these emails, so it might say, "Three lots left," or "This is my inventory home, it's available right now." How would I pre-template an email like this for three months from now? Three months from now pre-templated might be something that's a little bit less specific and might include, "Don't forget to file your homestead" or "How to read your property tax statement." Again, I don't think things like that will bring people in wanting to buy homes from you.

I am not saying that you should stop using your drip system. I am just saying for you to see it for what it is. It is a way to stay in the backs of the minds of everyone you've been in contact with. Only using a drip campaign to keep in touch with your current follow-up is too passive in my opinion. I typically use the drip campaigns for people who have already bought and closed and use constant contact for driving new traffic.

I'm not the used car dealer that's going to call you 20 times when you haven't called me back. I usually send off the first email within minutes of the first visit, make a phone call within three to five days to see if they have any follow up questions and also make sure they got my email if I haven't heard back from them. After that they're in my Constant Contact system. That may seem very limited, but I'm going to be honest; if you haven't called me back or you haven't emailed me back, there's probably a reason. Either I didn't deserve your business because I didn't do enough to earn it, which might change down the road, or you're just not interested in my product. There are a lot of people out there who will respond, focus on them.

Following up means walking a fine line between too little, where you're no longer in people's minds, and too much, where they unsubscribe because they think you're pestering them.

SmackDown

PART 3

Pulling it Together

CHAPTER 5
Lessons Learned

Over the years I have been doing this I have learned what to do and a lot of times what not to do. I've used these lessons to modify my actions, but there have also been a few things I've done that have just taken up a ton of time, and I never, no matter how differently I've done them, saw a return.

One of those is making my own website, maybe a community website, or something that was different from the website the company I worked for already had. I learned over time that all I'm doing is creating a competing online presence. Why try to take away from my parent company if their site can already do what I'm trying to accomplish? Why am I putting all my floor plan pictures up there if it's already on theirs? I can't build a web site better than theirs. There was never an organic traffic flow to those websites. It was just me saying, "Go to this."

Another "great idea" I had was creating a mail-out DVD. The idea behind it was that sometimes people came through the model, but I didn't have a chance to talk to about everything. I thought a presentation DVD would be perfect the thing to send. At the time, DVDs were the main method of watching video. My idea was, send a DVD to somebody. They'd think, "Wow, a DVD. I don't get DVDs in the mail all the time or ever really. Let's see what this is." Then, at that point, they'd watch it.

In theory it's a good idea, but now I can do the exact same thing with YouTube by just sending them a link, plus YouTube is free and free is always good. It's much easier, and YouTube links don't get thrown away in the trash or broken, like a DVD might. You can also track how many people have watched it, as opposed to DVDs.

I've experimented with a lot of things, and a lot of things have failed. Google Pay-Per-Click was one thing that I never saw as useful, and it's something you have to pay for. As I was using my own money, I had a very low tolerance for this. It needed to be blatantly successful for me to be willing to spend money on it. With Google Pay-Per-Click, in theory, you put in keywords and when people search for those keywords, your link comes up on the list of sponsored web pages. So, in theory, people who search for a new home will see your link and click on it. The problem is that all the big-name builders have paid much more than you have to be at the top of that list and for them to be there constantly. If you aren't spending a large amount of money you won't come up as a result in the search. I never had a single person come in, or a single person call me from this technique. In contrast I currently spend $20 or $30 and have hundreds of people, if not thousands of people, look at pictures I put up on Facebook. I couldn't get a single phone call, or email, or anything from Google Pay-Per-Click. People apparently clicked because I was spending money, but I just never saw any real return.

In almost everything else I've done, I've seen returns. I spend money on Constant Contact, Facebook, and flyers. I can tangibly see people walking into my model, or calling, or emailing me from these sources. There's a visible measurable result.

Sales Assistants

Interns and Assistants are an Extension of You. Whether you have an intern, assistant or a partner, both of you must have a clear and consistent message. This is something I've made a commitment to focus a little bit more on lately. If you and your partner or assistant have a different message when buyers walk into your model you basically start over each time someone comes back. They come back because of the experience they had previously, and you want to build on that each time they visit.

This message is basically your "USP" or your unique selling proposition. It boils down to one simple concept, what makes you different, what makes you better and why that should be important to your buyers. Instead of focusing on the boring things that everyone does, focus on what makes you special.

A lot of people have the mentality where, "If I train my assistant and teach them too much, they're going to end up leaving and going somewhere to get a full-time job." I don't see that as a negative thing. After all, which is worse? Having an assistant who leaves because you trained and mentored them, or having one who doesn't know anything, but is still working with you? That, to me, is the worst scenario.

CHAPTER 6

Summing it all up!

Using SmackDown for the First Time

As you put the SmackDown formula into play, what results might you expect?

If you remember from the introduction, I liken things to a water pump. Let's say you're pumping for water. You won't always see the water come up right away, but the more you pump, the more every action will create a reaction. The more you do, the more likely you're going to see results. If you do these things for a day or two, I seriously doubt you're going to see much of a difference. If you make a commitment to yourself to work on it for thirty days, then you might very well start seeing results.

Make the following commitment. **"I'm going to do more. I'm going to leave work every day knowing I did everything I possibly could. When I stand in a room of my peers, I will know I am the hardest working person in the room"**. If you do this for 30 days, I guarantee you there's nowhere you work that you won't see a difference.

As you finish this book, my advice to you is to read it again. The thing I've always done with books impact me the most, is to read through them or listen to them numerous times. You get something different every time you do. Reading the book again may help you formulate an idea of which of the things will work directly for you. You may also see what you could do slightly differently because your market's a maybe little bit different than mine.

Knowledge is never a bad thing. Take whatever knowledge and information you get, sift through what's important to you and put aside the stuff that isn't.

I always caution people not to discard things just because you don't think they will work. First find out if they will work. The more information there is, the more times you read it, the more likely you'll take something away from it. I encourage people to take notes, to highlight, to write down things they did or didn't do and how that worked better or maybe didn't work at all.

Summing it all up!

My main goal with this book is to help people. I've said time and time again; the main goal of this book is not to make money. If you've read this book and would like to move deeper into the SmackDown world and learn more, you can find us online at www.GetWillPower.com

You can contact us if you have questions or want to book a speaking event or talk with us about consulting work as well.

In closing, I leave you with this, which is one of the most impactful statements I've ever come across.

"You become what you think about."

The more you think about positivity, the more you think about what you want to become, and about what you want to happen the easier it is to achieve.

The more you surround yourself with positive people, the more you will become like them.

If you think about negative things constantly, or how things will go wrong and dwell on that, I believe you'll end up in that world. I've always believed in the fact that if you believe in something, you can go after it, and you can accomplish it, if you want it bad enough.

Made in the USA
Lexington, KY
05 September 2018